SMART MARKET FUTURE DEVELOPMENT

JOHN LOK

2018 Aug. Print Published

Contents

Preface

Introduction

I write this book aims to let readers to feel that future artificial intelligent (AI) technology whether it could be applied to which aspects to satisfy our life need. I shall concentrate on predicting (AI) technology can be applied to these several aspects: education, business, transportation, space tourism, medical health these five aspects. This is my opinion, it is not absolute true. However, I shall follow our nowadays (AI) technological development trend to explain how I predict how (AI) technology will be invented to applied to these five aspects to satisfy consumer individual and businessman individual both needs, even I shall explain how to (AI) tool to predict consumer behavior in psychological function successfully.. However, I shall explain why (AI) manufacturers need to concern ethic matter, if they do not concern ethic or moral matter, any future (AI) industry development will be encountered failure. So, I bring this two questions:Why do ethic or moral matter is important to influence any (AI) industry development success? What will be caused negative influence to (AI) consumer comsumption desire if any (AI) manufacturers do not concern (AI) ethic or moral matter?

First part, I shall explain how and why (AI) technology can be applied to space exploration missions and space tourism development. Will artificial intelligent space exploration bring long term economic , entertainment and technological benefits? What factors will apply (AI) technology to assist space tourism leisure development? How to apply (AI) technology to solve any challenges during space travelling boats fly to space to encounter sudden accident.

This part concerns whether artificial intelligent technology can be used in future space development. Firstly, I shall explain how human can apply artificial intelligent technology to space development which aspects. Then, I shall indicate how scientists need to follow what steps in order to achieve (AI) space robotic technology can be used in space technology to develop more successful. In this part, I shall also explain what benefits or strengths that (AI) space robotic technology can bring to assist space development as well as what disadvantages or weaknesses if (AI) space robotic technology can not be used to assist space development.

Second part, I shall explain how future (AI) technology can be applied to business and health service aspect. Can AI grow productivity?

If AI can grow productivity, how can it raise ? If productivity raised, can it raise economic development ? How will (AI) influence human job change? It brings this question: Which (AI) workers be instead of traditional human workers in these different new markets? In recent years, machines had been used to be human's tasks in the performance of certain tasks related to intelligence , such as aspects of image recognition. Experts also forecast that rapid progress in the field of specialized artificial intelligence will continue. Then, it also brings this question: Does (AI) exceed that of human performance on more and more tasks? If it is truth, will some of human jobs to be disappeared? (AI) will be instead of human some simple jobs, then unemployment rate to the low skillful and low educated workers will be increased.

This part concerns to be given my opinions to explain whether artificial intelligent technology will impact our life and will influence economic development in the future, due to productivity raises.

This third part aims to explain how to apply artificial intelligent machine men to teach students in University. If one day, artificial intelligent machine men can be invent to own human's mind and judgement abilities. I believe that universities can attempt to apply artificial intelligent machine men to teach students in lecturer hall. When, artificial intelligent machine men can be invented to learn how to reading any books, writing any books, learning any subject

knowledge, even learn how to make judgement to answer any students studying challenges. Then, it is possible that they can be applied to replace universities lecturers their teaching jobs to teach students in univeristy hall.
In this third part, I shall assume when artificial intelligent machine men can learn how to write books and/or read books. Then, they will have human's mind ability in possible. Can future artificial intelligent machine men be invented to learn how to write books and/or read books ability? In my this book, I shall attempt to answer this question. Finally, I hope my readers can attempt to make judgement whether artificial intelligent machine men can really learn how to write and read books to do lecturer's teaching job. In the future, AI technology can be applied to education industry. It will be one new technological popular education tool to assist university teachers to teach their students after the human lecturers had taught their teaching subject contents to let them to remember before every time lecturing teaching in lecture hall. To explain how AI technological technology can be apply to developing countries in Asia, e.g. Philippines, Korea, China, US, UK etc. developed countries to replace human lecturers to teach their students popularly. The benefits of AI machine teaching lecturer can assist human lecturer to teach students in lecturing halls, then human lecturers can concentrate on researching jobs.

In this fourth part, This part brings readers to image what will be different if artificial intelligent non manual driving vehicle will be used to public transportation and private transportation both aspects in popular. I shall explain why AI safety system will be successful factor to influence future non-manual transportation successful development. Will it popular to accept to use any artificial intelligent vehicles? Is it possible to apply AI non-manual driving technology to AI non-manual driving transportation tools global transportation market? For example, in (AI) non-manual vehicle industry, driving automatic vehicle whether it will be accepted to drivers who have confidence to drive it on roads safely. Whether artificial (AI) intelligent non-manual driving systems are the improvement of traffic safety, reduction of energy consumption or improvement of the comfort of the driver.

Whether will it be popular to accept to apply artificial intelligent non-manual driving technology from non-manual auto driving cars to be applied to any non-manual auto driving transportation tools transportation market development, such as train, tram, lorry, transportation air plane, passenger air plane, ferry, taxi, MTR. Etc. different kinds of transportation tools? If future human accepts to use any non-manual driving vehicles or non-manual driving transportation tools, what advantages and disadvantages will bring to influence our daily life. How if (AI) non-manual auto driving technology stage is mature to achieve non-manual driving technology is safe driving. It is possible that (AI) non-manual driving cars can influence to change whole manual driving transportation tools to non-manual driving transportation tools. How it will influence (AI) autonomous cars change to influence global manual driving transportation industry development ?

In fifth part, I shall explain how to apply (AI) tool to attempt to predict consumer behavior in travelling industry, this part has these two research questions need to be answered. Can apply (AI) learning machine predict travelling consumer behavior? Can (AI) big data gathering learning machine be replaced to human travelling marketing research method, e.g. survey or traveler psychological and travelling marketing research or travelling environment micro and macro economic human judgement of traveler consumption behavior prediction methods to predict travelling consumer behaviors more accurate?

In this part, I concentrate on explain why artificial intelligence (AI) big data gathering tool will be one kind of good traveler consumer behavioral prediction tool to be chose to apply to predict traveler consumer consumption behavior concerns when and why and how their travelling behavior will change. I shall indicate some cases examples to give reasonable evidences to analyze whether (AI) big data gathering tool will be one kind suitable tool to be applied to predict when and how and why travelling consumer behavioral changes. If (AI) big data can be one kind tool to attempt to be applied to predict when and how and why travelling consumer behavioral changes. Will it make more accurate to compare otherkinds of methods to predict travelling consumerbehaviors, e.g. survey, telephone questionnaire? Does it have weaknesses tobe applied to predict travelling consumer behaviors, instead of strengths? Can it be applied to predict travelling consumer behaviors depending on any situations or only some situations?

In final part, I shall explain why although artificial intelligence (AI) technology is popular to be applied to different industry aspects, such as medical, construction, transportation, hospital, education etc. Although, (AI) is a human invention new development. IN fact, it seems only beneficial to human's daily life. But, it will also have threats to influence human's safety in possible , if some scientists or self-interest mind people who aim to apply (AI) to earn more profit or apply (AI) tools to be weapon to attack other countries to achieve to dominate all human's ambitious intention. Thus, (AI) will bring negative influences to our society, instead of positive influences if we can not apply this kind of new technological tools immorally. In this final part, I shall give my opinions to indicate what reasons will cause (AI) artificial intelligent tools to be applied to social military defense weapon by human's intention. In this part, I hope my readers can know what will cause human's immoral behaviors to bring our societies to bring more dangerous or risks or threats if human applied (AI) technology to achieve whose immoral or ambitious intention. Finally, I hope that human ought not apply (AI) technology to do any behavioral attack to satisfy ourselves interest or dominate global world ambition to avoid (AI) technological war occurrence in the future one day.

Prologue

Table of content

- What (AI) functionis? Can (AI) impact human job nature? p.182-192
- How can (AI) influence labor market?
- How can human society job nature to be changed to artificial intelligent society?
- Why does human need artificial intelligence machines?

- How does artificial intelligence influence future working changing in automation employment and productivity aspects?

- Is artificial intelligence possible to replace labor ?
- Can (AI) technology replace human labour nature of work?
- Why can artificial intelligence satisfy human needs?
- Is artificial intelligence one good choice for human future technological benefit?

(AI) technological Space exploration missions

ONE

HOW ARTIFICIAL INTELLIGENT TECHNOLOGY CONTROL SYSTEMS ARE USED IN SPACE

In the future, space intelligent control systems can be applied to space in these aspects:

Firstly, in space communication aspect, when spacecraft have a special need for (AI) system, due to communication delays and other factors, much of (AI) control system development is conducted for earth-based applications. As a result, (AI) communication system can let spacemen communicate to earth space station staffs between of them more easy and in short time communication in possible.

Additionally, ground support systems are required to facilitate communication with and command of (AI) controlled and other spacecraft. Future, numerous successful missions or which are controlled by (AI) technology have been launched. Thus, future many space missions seem to be controlled by (AI) control systems are better than none or lacked (AI) control systems assistance.

Secondly, in space exploration aspect, in the future, it is possible that fully autonomous spacecraft control has been confirmed in a limited capacity and appears to build promise for reducing any space exploration mission cost, increasing scientific returns and allowing the operation of more complex multi-vehicle missions from possible future of artificial intelligence control systems in space. Thus, future it is possible that (AI) control systems can been automated to assist any space scientists to solve problem during their each space exploration process.

Thirdly, in automated ground based testing system aspect, in the future autonomous spaceflight will start on the ground. For each spacecraft that is sent into space to explore, numerous concepts must be proposed, developed and tested on earth to ensure a successful mission.

Can future (AI) control systems be developed to be applied to automated test any spacecraft flight systems to ensure which are safe to leave earth to fly to space? Is (AI) automated system testing tool more accurate to achieve the testing safe measurement result to reduce the space flight risk than human testing effort? To answer these questions, scientists need to attempt to compare (AI) testing system and human effort to test many times of spacecraft flights in order to confirm whether (AI) testing system will be more accurate than human effort testing to every spacecraft equipment before it will fly to space.

Fourthly, in autonomous space exploration problem solution aspect, when a spacecraft encountered a somewhat unique problem as it moves further and further from earth. The increasing distance makes it take from ground-based controllers. As such, a spacecraft that will be any significant distance from earth most have some problems need to be able take collision avoidance actions and to reestablish communications with earth should they are lost.

The use of (AI) autonomous technologies started with meeting these basic requirements and performing actions (such as docking), which required too much. However, (AI) technology will have possible to be implemented because it can make missions better and less expensive. When, (AI) technology is participated to solve any unpredictable challenges when any a spacecraft leaves our earth to fly to space for future mission plans. It is likely the future existing space site networks will expand and some of which may be in remote locations. As such, there is an even greater need for (AI) automated challenge solution technology to facilities the operation of these various space stations within budget.

Consequently, future (AI) technology can be used in space on communication, space exploration, automated ground based testing, autonomous space exploration problem solution aspects. Nowadays, human is waiting when (AI) technology can be invented to assist space development, such as the day comes.

1.1 Challenges to install (AI) automated system in space stations

I shall indicate one challenge case how Earth space station installs (AI) automated control system to assist future any each spacecraft to achieve lot missions more productive and efficient. Ton install (AI) automated control system, which will follow two challenge views to achieve in success as below:

The first challenge view aims to apply (AI) automated system to increase the quality and productivity of each space mission current experience. However, proponents of this challenge viewpoint believed that the (AI) expert system should be developed to allow and experienced operator to make better flight decisions. They do not believe future (AI) artificial intelligent automated control system can make more accurate decisions or operator to reduce or avoid sudden accident occurrence chances during their every space mission trip.

However, (AI) automated control system scientists believed that this could be done by developing a (AI) automated control system capable of continuously analyzing all incoming telemetry to a depth that would be impractical ever for an experienced operator.

Moreover, the (AI) automated control system scientists felt that the potential dollar value of this (AI) space automated control system investment is difficult to quantify. They indicated that a single good decision which allowed completion of a several hundred million dollar mission would clearly pay for a large amount of (AIO automated control system work, but it is difficult to say that the good decision was completely the result of the expert system.

Developing an (AI) space station expert system needs to meet this goal, such as : Reducing every time space mission flight accident occurrence as well as assisting human space flight operators to control spacecraft equipment to raise every space mission trip efficiency and productivity. So, it requires the incorporation of deep knowledge about a given spacecraft monitoring task.

Hence, the first challenge to (AI) expert system to be how to install to space stations, it is the unpredictable (AI) expert system investment amount spending and lacked depth knowledge skill of personnel each (AI) expert operator. It is only one (AI) expert system research stage to future space stations. It still needs time to research how to invent (AI) automated control system to assist space stations to implement productivity and efficiency as well as deducing space accident occurrence chances to future every space mission.

The second challenge view was how to use (AI) expert systems to allow each less experienced space flight personnel operator to perform at the level of more senior personnel. That has a measurable cost benefit that it allows shorter training times. This viewpoint requires an emphasis on breadth of knowledge as well as improved human-computer interfaces. Thus, the second challenge is unsure achievement of shorter training times measurement to assist less experienced personnel space flight operators from (AI) space expert systems assistance to achieve shorter training time productivity and efficiency aim.

Consequently, (AI) experts need to solve these two challenges to avoid space station operators feel worries whether (AI) technology can really help them to work in order to achieve (AI) automated operation control system achievement to space stations installation implementation for every space mission plan in success.

TWO

Chapter 2

How can artificial intelligence be applied to adapt the nature of space and satellite industry

The nature of the space and satellite industry how to require machine intelligence and assistance to launch, operate, maintain, control, repair and ensure achievement of any space missions. Some examples of potential (AI) application include as below:

(1) Remote sensing and monitoring to predict how and when space environment changes, spacecraft security, and space mission location or destination tracking.

(2) Communications between ground and space as well as from satellite-to-satellite (in the case of multi-satellite stations), using radio frequencies, optical -laser communications, radar along with growing complexity of satellite-to-satellite handoffs between satellites in different orbits.

(3) Robotics in space transportation, include mission extension vehicles, space docking, satellite health monitoring manned space vehicles support(including health safety, medical , analytics, repair) and spacecraft to make their own decisions to explore, learn, identify, adapt during missions and carry out repairs.

(4) Data analytics include gathering large amounts of information and how that information can be used from national security , data privacy to assist space mission organizations to carry on any future space research analyses.

(5) Reusable launch and manned vehicles include sophisticated (AI) for return to Earth for completion of mission, e.g. researching asteroid mining resource includes analytics of substances discerned from asteroid examples, and remote mining of the same.

(6) Remote missions to Mars or Moon planets and beyond (and a board variety of information transit, and return). Satellites as alternative to terrestrial-based systems include cloud computing, cross-border broadband services, and other multi-data and information transfer.

2.1 What is (AI) unmanned aircraft system?

Unmanned aircraft system is a kind of commercial transportation tool to provide benefits in terms of safety and efficiency to carry on implementing future every flight space mission aim. Advances in (AI) and machine learning technology are allowing it to see and act like human pilots, and to process huge amounts of data in real time search and rescue missions, e.g. allowing farmers to be more efficient and environmentally friendly inspecting power lives and cell tower, survey and mapping of land or performing package delivery searching job duties. (AI) is allowing more automated , safer and efficient in Earth land, e.g. farming land and space planets' land, e.g. Mars, Moon planets.

The applications of (AI) in Earth or space land data gathering industry are limited only be data analytics for space or Earth land industrial inspections to navigating, future space warehouses more efficiently to assist spacecraft operators to transport any things between space warehouses easily in any space planets ' lands.

2.2 Real-time data analytics

(AI) can collect and process huge volumes of data in real time. For example, gathering space environment or space planet land imagery that is used to take humans' hours, days or weeks to review and analyze is being automated by (AI) that strategically determines that kind of data and images are important enough to collect, and can simulate a human looking a lot of any space images in short time clearly. For example, when one spacecraft needs to perform inspections whether its inside machines or equipment which parts to be needed to repair, due to they are sudden damaged in any non-predictive accident event during the space mission journey. Then , it can use a variety of onboard sensors (AI cameras) to inspect track conditions and identify defects that are invisible in the spacecraft. Once detected, (AI) robots can be used to provide recommendations on what, if any maintenance may be necessary.

2.3 (AI) robotic detective system

(AI) robotic detective system can assist spacecraft to avoid obstacles, such as space stones sudden collision in non-predictive space environment, when space stones are flying toward to it suddenly. So, (AI) robotic detective system can be capable of any flying autonomously space stones with human intention, and this will require (AI) robotic detective system to help the spacecraft to have able to sense when the space stones obstacles will fly toward to the spacecraft direction and react in time to avoid a collision. Hence, computer plus (AI) machine learning is helping any spacecraft navigate more effectively in dangerous space environment. (AI) robots are enabling the spacecraft will fly safely, even in dark, space stones obstacle filled space environment or beyond the obstacle reaches of GPS or other methods of Earth stations communication connectivity in dangerous space environment,

2.4 The ethic challenges to (AI) space robotic learning system in space environment application

Firstly, space environment situational awareness challenge, (AI) needs have enable better space environment situational awareness and changing the ways are able to interact with things in any dangerous space environment. In the not-too distant future, (AI) technology will enable fully autonomous operations. So, (AI) space robots have ultimate safe responsibility to every spacecraft operators on aircrafts and on the human spacecraft pilots, when they depend on (AI) space robots to assist them to work in dangerous space environment.

(AI) space robots have responsibility to assist spacecraft operators and spacecraft pilots to make accurate judgement. It will raise important policy questions regarding the removal of human judgement from the (AI) space robot's judgement. Human spacecraft pilots make not only safety-related decisions, but in certain circumstances, especially emergencies, moral and ethical decisions, such as whether to crash space rocks sudden fly toward to the spacecraft. So, (AI) space robots will be needed to learn from space flight experience and use that learned knowledge to make appropriate moral and ethical judgements in dangerous space environment.

Hence, it brings this question: Do spacecraft pilots or/and spacecraft operators or (AI) space robots have legal responsibilities to maintain the security of any space mission flight as well as to ensure that its automation, space navigation, and space communication systems are good to be used?

So, (AI) space robots bring with its significant new issues involving (AI) spacecraft automated control system product liability, data privacy, intellectual property. The bound liability issues for risk and/or space mission business model includes allocation of responsibilities and costs for compliance between the spacecraft pilots/spacecraft operators and (AI) automated control system itself.

The standard allocation of known or anticipated risks between parties will separate provisions for allocating unknown rocks through on every space mission flight. Thinking these issues , through it is critical, and it may b e to (AI) space robots and spacecraft operators/ space pilots advantage to set cost and liabilities expectations, rather than to later dispute resolution. All reasonable scenarios should be approved when every space mission trip is planned to implement.

THREE

ARTIFICIAL INTELLIGENT ROBOTIC SPACE MISSION OR SPACE TOURISM STRATEGY

When one space exploration or space tourism organization can have one good strategic plan, it will have more accurate effort to predict either space tourism consumer individual leisure behavior or space exploration mission more successful. However to achieve artificial intelligence technology strategy to any space exploration mission or space tourism?

I believe that artificial intelligence technology strategy to natural language, transportation, client service, education etc. (AI) businesses implementation. It must be different to artificial intelligence space exploration mission or space tourism businesses implementation. However, artificial intelligence space exploration mission and space tourism both strategies, which will be similar , due to which concerns how to apply artificial intelligent technology to achieve spacecraft for space exploration mission or space tourism how to raise efficiency and productivity and avoid or reduce space stones collision accident occurrence chances in dangerous space environment.

Hence, space tourism or space exploration mission organizations need to concern above these aspects to implement their strategic plan. So, we know that the strategic plan for artificial intelligence technology to be applied to space exploration missions or space tourism missions which aims to help space operators and space pilots to make predictive judgement to reduce or avoid sudden space accident, e.g. space stones collision to the spacecraft to cause space operators or space pilots hurt, even die as well as how to apply artificial intelligence to assist space operators/space pilots to raise efficiency, when they are carrying on any space exploration missions or space tourism leisure missions.

3.1 How to achieve artificial intelligence technology to space exploration mission or space tourism mission more easier and more effective?

I recommend pace tourism or space exploration mission organizations can set up one examination structure of strategic council for (AI) technology to assist space exploration mission or space tourism development. When the strategic council for (AI) technology was established the (AI) research coordination council and space industry coordination council were also needed to be researched.

The (AI) coordination council needs to be progressed with giving shape to linkages in (AI) research and development carried out by there ministries. The space exploration mission or space tourism industry coordination council needs to carry out surveys and investigations on (1) establishing a roadmap for space exploration or space tourism industrialization, (2) fostering of space operators, space pilots, space tourism leisure customer service operator of human resources, (3) data maintenance/provision and open tools, (4) measures, such as for fostering start-ups and financial linkages, in aiming towards how to apply (AI) technology to assist any space exploration mission or space tourism research and development carried out more easily.

With regard to ethical aspects of (AI) technology to space tourism or space exploration mission, intellectual property right, personal information protection and promotion of open data, separate opportunities for examine whether the (AI) strategic plan is suitable to the space tourism leisure business or space exploration mission business. If the organization feel it is not suitable to the space tourism leisure or space exploration mission business. Then , it can attempt to find what weaknesses are for its (AI) strategic plan and to revise to correct its (AI) strategic plan more easier.

The (AI) strategic plan can concern how to apply (AI) industry roadmap technology to assist to related space exploration or space tourism technologies . Thus, the (AI) strategic plan includes new (AI) automated control system assistance service and space robotic products to be utilized and applied of (AI) technology to spacecraft technology. It aims to avoid or reduce sudden accident occurrences and it can predict when and how and why sudden accident occurrences as well as how to solve these challenges urgently during the spacecraft is flying on the space environment.

Hence, the strategic plan of (AI) technology must assist human space pilots/space operators to raise any space exploration missions or space tourism missions efficiency and it must assist them to predict when sudden accidents will happen, e.g. predicting when and where space rocks collision to the spacecraft in order to avoid the accident occurrences in space environment.

The (AI) strategic plan can include these three phases to any space tourism or space exploration missions in space industry. (AI) technology is simply a service to be provided to space operators/ space pilots to use to assist them to make more efficient and reduce or avoid sudden accident occurrence chances in space environment. The three phases are as below:

(1) The first phase: Utilization and application of data-driven (AI) automated control systems/ space robots developed in the space

environment. This phase aims to achieve space (AI) automated control systems and / space robots to raise space service efficiency.

● On real-time assessment of space

On operator operational status hand, it includes such as below: How to use space robots on any unmanned space tasks assistance to space operators / space pilots? How to predict when failure of space equipment damage occurrence and how to solve those sudden accident occurrence challenges in spacecraft during it is flying gin space environment? How to apply (AI) -based prediction / matching of supply and demand to every spacecraft its space exploration mission or space tourism trip need, such as on-demand space (AI) robotic assistance supply service, optimization control of spacecraft energy consumption by using (AI) automated control energy management system technology, cooperative space tasks by human space operators/space pilots and space robots, implementation of space robots that simulate behavior of space pilots and space pilots, enhancement of space operators / space pilots cooperation with space (AI) robots? Which aims to create of new cooperation services with space (AI) robots / space (AI) automation control systems assistance in order to achieve any space tasks more efficient, reducing / avoiding any sudden space accident occurrence chances from manual or non-predictive space environment factors.

(2) The second phase: Space robots able to perform multiple functions and cooperate with each other to assist space operators or space pilots to do different tasks in the spacecraft, creation of diversified space robotic services.

(3) The third phase: It is the final strategic plan stage. It aims to achieve any space exploration missions / space tourism leisure missions which can achieve innovative space services and space (AI) robots are continuously developed to assist space operators / space pilots to do different tasks efficiently and effectively in shorten time, during they are carrying on any tasks in any spacecraft.

The final phase of space strategic plan objectives include as below:

● Space (AI) robots can assist to space operators / space pilots to solve manual task errors discovery in order to help human space pilots / space operators to solve challenges in any time in spacecraft.

● Space robots that can provide walking assistance, supervision, and support through conversation to cooperate with space pilots / space operators to attempt to solve challenges in any time in spacecraft.

● Space robots which can understand the space operator / space pilots intentions or needs how to finish or do every task or space mission efficiently and effectively.

● Space robots can collect of space traveler individual information and predict of when space environment will change using (AI) space robots and sensors. For example, space robots can take 3 D maps or photos , when they need to be assisted to take any space exploration mission photos on Mars or Moon etc. planet lands.

● Diversification of spatial space transportation vehicle devices, such as (AI) space vehicle drones assist space operators to deliver cargos / carriages on any planet lands.

● Diversification of space transportation devices, providing valuable space transportation service for space travelers.

Consequently, (AI) space strategic plan aims to let space operators lead space robots / space operation control systems can follow these three phases (stages), in order to have right or reasonable direction to let space operators, space pilots, space tourism service operators, space exploration mission operators who can also follow right or reasonable direction to achieve whose space tourism leisure aim or space exploration mission more easier and efficient from (AI) technology assistance.

(AI) robotic technology brings long term or short term benefits to space exploration industry

Whether do scientists spend time and money to invest artificial intelligent invention to space exploration industry, is it worth to earn short term benefits only ? As NASA exploration moves beyond earth's orbit, the need excites for long duration space systems that are needed to ensure events that compromise safety and performance. I believe that the (AI) technology advances in autonomy, robotic manipulators, artificial intelligent in-space vehicles can provide service possible at acceptance cost and risk.

I shall explain how to evaluate future space systems needed to support scientific observatories and human/robotic Mar, Moon planets exploration to access key structure design considerations. How can impact of in-space robots, (AI), in-space vehicles to support NASA's future long duration missions?

(1) Robotic in-space vehicle

In the future, new knowledge is gained by robotic scientific observatories like the Hubble space telescope and the Mars covers will have result to be applied to commercial and government spacecraft launch needs. Why do future space exploration missions need (AI) technological assistance? The reasons include improving aperture size, decreasing deployment risk, such as assembling systems are too large to fit into a single in-space launch vehicle and enabling repair and upgrade easily if any future space exploration missions choose to apply (AI) technological assistance. It will reduce cost and accident occurrence risks.

In this Mars exploration case, NASA's science and exploration missions of the future require spacecraft systems, both robotic and human tended, they can cooperate in deep space for extended provider of time. The Mars exploration mission could used (AI) tools to assist human space operators to test deep space habitation technologies for a Mars transport habitat. The robotic in-space vehicles could also be repurposed as an exploration platform surface exploration and provides a deep space vehicle assembly and servicing site in Mars. So, the robotic in-space vehicles can assist space operators to deliver cargos in Mars, different space sites.

Moreover, the space (AI) in-space robots have also these advantages, such as free-flyer robots which can fly to Mars different space sites to observe Mars different space sites situations to find whether what needs they need to assist, fuel storage function repair and assembly function, long reach manipulators functions power / data / mechanical joining technology function, high power, mass efficiency, large scientific observatories function.

Hence, future robotic in-space vehicle tool which can assist space operators to observe Mars different space sites easily, transport any cargos on Mars different sites between them easily. Even, it can assist space operators to attempt to find whether where has water resource, and find suitable farming land locations grow food to provide human to eat in Mars, and find alive existing locations in possible. Thus, space robotic in-space vehicle is a good example to assist space operators to achieve future Mars exploration mission for long term time.

(2) Robotic spacecraft

In the future, the first space robots will possible be spacecraft and probes and the main goals of these machines was the Moon or Mars surface aiming manned missions to the Earth natural satellite. The capability of these robotic spacecraft included photographing and recording the surface and sending television images to the Earth.

The first robotic spacecraft will send to the Moon had not even the capability to land in the surface. They were lunar impact robotic spacecraft. Television images were obtained and send to the Earth when falling down on the Moon. Other robotic space achievements by using probes were directed to Nenus, Mars and Mercury, Jupiter and Saturn.

However, space robotic spaceship will face these challenges to be solve if space scientists expect future space robotic spaceships can attempt to fly to Moon, even other planets to reach these any one of space planet destinations successfully.

The challenges include that it supposes the space journey needs to reach the space region with Voyager 1 and the most distant planets with Voyager 2. The robots are needed to be the appropriate machines to substitute the astronauts in risky activities in the non-predictive dangerous space environment. How to design the artificial intelligent robot will be more important and will be a key issue for the future of space exploration?

The orbital robot requires to solve these problems , such as radiation, strong temperature variation, micro-gravity environment and magnetic fields associated to some celestial bodies. Specially, for planetary exploration aspect of the robotic application includes surface exploration where the local gravity, soil characteristics, local pressure and atmosphere must be consideration. So, future space robotic tool development still needs to find solutions to deal these above challenges when it brings to space environment to be used.

(3) Space navigation and long distant mobility

In the future space stations need have robots to help them to repair when sudden accident occurrences to cause any one of space stations' machines to be damaged. In-space operations involve operations functionalities like in-space assembly, in-space inspection, in-space maintenance, extra-vehicular activities, and in-orbit scientific experiment. For example, planetary exploration robotic applications are remarkably operating on Mar surface.

Space scientists predict the next 10 years, it is expected that the space robots for surface exploration be not constrained anymore by, navigation and long distance mobility to access to most locations on a planetary surface will be possible. On the other side, it is expected that ground based planning and visualization tools enable scientists from space ground station to interact with the space robots in the surface of celestial bodies. However, robotic performance at the level of a space suited human scientist is and will continue to be a major challenge.

Anyway, the automation by using robots in space operation will bring the advent of space stations and orbital service. One of the most important accomplishment with an extraordinary space robot was the space shuttle series of spacecraft. Space shuttle can be considered future first space robotic shuttle can be provided series of spacecraft service. Thus, future space robotic shuttle can be considered in that if really implemented orbital servicing of grasping satellite for maintenance, and assembly for the international space station and inserting new satellite into low Earth orbit.

Consequently, robotic technology can bring long term benefits to any space exploration missions. It is absolute short term benefits. For example, robotic vehicles can assist space operators to deliver cargos in long distance between different space stations fast and easily. They don't need manual control. Such as on Mars or Moon planets which will let many robotic vehicles move on their lands to move lot of building materials to build houses or space stations or space warehouses or space laboratories on Mars between different space sites. The benefits are that they do not need space operators drive them to more on Mars lands. They can move on Mars land automatically. So, space operators can concentrate on doing their space exploration tasks.

For another example, space robots can take 3D photo images in Mars easily. They can deliver 3D photo images more clear and visible in short time from Mars on Moon planet to Earth space stations. They do not need space operators to control, they can automate to take 3D clear photo of Mars or Moon current images more clear in order to let Earth space station scientists to see these visible 3D Mars or Moon planets images to gather data to prepare to do any space exploration missions immediately as soon as possible.

For final example, future space robots can learn space operators to attempt to assist them to do any maintenance tasks. So, when the aircraft encounters sudden accident to cause machine (equipment) damage, then the space robots can assist to the space operators to find the damaged equipment to repair immediately. So, they can share space operators' maintenance tasks risks if human operators feel difficult to find which are the damaged equipment which need to be repaired. Then, space robots has possible to find which are the damaged equipment to be repaired immediately. Hence, future space robotic technology seems to bring long term benefits to any exploration missions absolutely.

(AI) technological Space tourism

FOUR

FUTURE SPACE TOURISM PSYCHOLOGY PREDICTION STRATEGY

● Psychology and economic environment changing both factors influence whole space tourism market leisure desire

How can apply (AI) technological and psychology method to attract future space tourism customer individual space tourism desire? I believe that it has relationship between the space tourism planner and the safe (AI) space tourism environment to attract every one space tourism passenger to catch the (AI) space boat to fly to space to travel as below:

Firstly,the space travelling planner individual psychology influence hand, the space travelling planner will have these both aspects of individual psychological influence, it includes these both either positive or negative psychological influence aspectsas below:

On the positive psychological influence aspect, if the space travelling planner has confidence to the space travelling leisure company can provide safe, comfortable, good quality of one space travelling trip arrangement, good taste food arrangement, reasonable space ticket price and every reasonable space trip for space hotel living arrangement and space garden and space farming land visiting journey arrangement, even, space swimming pool and space sport centre and space cinema leisure arrangement to let whom to stay on the planet at least one day trip, it means not one short time space trip, e.g. the spacecraft only flies about half hour or one half. It can not fly to the planet to arrive its space station destination to stay to let the space travelling planner to live at the space hotel at least one night. Then the space travelling planner will have more desire to choose to catch the space tourism leisure company's spacecraft to travel to space.

Secondly, on the negative psychological influence aspect, if the space travelling planner lacks confidence to the space travelling leisure company can provide safe, comfortable, good quality of one space travelling trip arrangement, good taste food arrangement, reasonable space ticket price and every reasonable space trip for space hotel living arrangement and space garden and space farming land visiting journey arrangement, even, space swimming pool and space sport centre and space cinema leisure arrangement to let whom to stay on the planet at least one day trip, it means not one short time space trip, e.g. the spacecraft only flies about half hour or one half. It can not fly to the planet to arrive its space station destination to stay to let the space travelling planner to live at the space hotel at least one night. Then the space travelling planner will have less desire to choose to catch the space tourism leisure company's spacecraft to travel to space.

Hence, it seems safe (AI) technological space boat factor and the space travelling planner's confidence factor to the space tourism leisure providers will influence the whole space travelling market whose space travelling consumer's space travelling leisure consumption desire to be more or less. So, any one space tourism provider will need to consider how to apply (AI) technology to assist space boat safety how to influence whose customer consumption desire.

● space tourism strategy

Future any space tourism leisure business needs have good business plan to outline the space tourism leisure business in these aspects , such as: different space tourism destinations of every space tourism journey, technical , financial and regulatory factors for growing space tourism leisure consumption into any one kind of unique artificial intelligent space tourism journey for identified passenger target group.

All how to design one space tourism business development plan to attempt to predict whether what trends will influence how every different kinds of identified space tourism journey in order to achieve passenger number growing aim as well as how to achieve one attractive space tourism leisure to satisfy future space tourism passenger individual space travel needs more easily.

I shall indicate what aspects to future every space tourism traveler who will consider in order to reduce the space tourism traveler personal worry to catch any pace boats to leave our Earth to fly to other planets to travel.

I recommend that any space tourism leisure organizations need to concern how to to apply (AI) technology to these aspects in their space tourism leisure business plan as below:

(1) safe space tourism journey

On first aspect concerns safe space tourism journey plan to let all space tourism travelers will considerate safe issue. They must ensure space boats that is safe to catch them to fly to planets in their space journeys. So, any space tourism leisure business will utilize previous flight rated and proven technologies to form the basis for manufacturing spacecraft vehicles, and will incorporate the latest modern avionics and flight systems for ensuring safety, reliability and economical operation in order to reduce any space tourism traveler personal worry to catch any spacecraft.

So, the space tourism safe journey plan is one very important factor to influence space tourism consumer number for them if any one of space tourism leisure business hoped they can grow the space tourism consumer number for long term. For example, the space boat flight hardware must often be maintained at the space station. It is needed to be considered by space boat experts as risky, extremely expensive and potentially sensitive. To aims to ensure spacecraft will offer an economical and safe alternative for any satellite manufacturers and other space tourism entertainment organizations have a desire or requirement for space tourism flight.

(2) reduction cost expense plan

On second aspect concerns reduction cost expense plan, any space tourism entertainment organizations need have the experience and capacity for safely launching a fully loaded , including space tourism passengers and passenger individual cargo for every spacecraft tourism journey. As a result of outsourcing the launch role to a major contractor, the space tourism pilot can concentrate on space boat crews flight training, planning space tourism passenger cargo capacity and preparing space flight manifests , and will as a result, avoid the expense of maintaining a launch operation on a daily basis.

In addition, by outsourcing the spacecraft manufacturing, it can avoid spending millions of dollar on facilities and equipment infrastructure and engineering manufacturing expertise.

(3) achieve any space tourism mission plan

On third aspect concerns how to achieve any space tourism mission. Every space tourism mission must be ensure that reliable service is provided to satisfy every space tourism passenger personal space traveler needs and let them to enjoy in their whole space tourism journey, let them to catch a big aircraft in comfortable environment of technologically sophisticated space boat, reasonable and competitive every time space tourism flight ticket price plan is developed and properly revised every time space tourism ticket

price when performing their assigned every different space tourism journey mission.
Hence, the space tourism leisure company will provide one careful selected space tourism destination , e.g. Mar planet space tourism journey, Moon planet space tourism journey or no any space destination journey, it means that the space craft only needs to fly one circle around between Earth and Moon space journey etc. that are capable of meeting the requirements of travelling into Earth orbit. So, any space tourism journey must emphasize affordability, reliability, safety, customer service and responsiveness in responding to every client's space tourism journey requirements. Hence, any one of space tourism journey must have clear space journey mission and objective to satisfy any space traveler client target needs.

FIVE

Methods to Raise Space Traveler Number

Future space tourism will be one kind of new travel leisure market for any new space travel leisure companies to enter this undiscovered market in the beginning. However, how to predict future 10 to 20 years , even more space traveler number that is one important issue to any new space tourism leisure companies.

I think that space tourism leisure companies need to apply (AI) technology to define what kinds of space travel leisure service to be provided to space travelling passengers, however, what age group of space passengers who will be their space travelling target client. For example, their space travel leisure must provide any flight operation that takes one or more passengers beyond the altitude of 100 km and thus into space to let space travelling passengers who have fun, exciting space travelling feeling.

Anyway, for any kind of space tourism (leisure space travel) journey, space tourism leisure company needs anyone to be bring customer satisfaction, it is a plan or predictive methods to measure how to let every space travelling passenger to feel comfortable when they are catching the spacecraft (space flying product) and they can have enjoyable and fun or exciting feeling when they have need providing any space tourism journey, services meet or surpass customer expectations.

Thus, any space tourism leisure company needs to evaluate the degree of every time space tourism journey's customer satisfaction and customer satisfaction is also always evaluated in relationship to the every time ticket price of the space tourism journey. So, the space tourism leisure company will predict the next time of what the space tourism journey of passenger number is more accurate, after it has evaluated what degree of every time space tourism journey's customer satisfaction is. It aims to gather their opinions to find which aspects that they need to revise, e.g. choosing where will be the next time space tourism journey destination, how to improve spacecraft staff's service attitude and performance to serve to their space tourism passengers when they are catching the spacecraft, to evaluate whether the spacecraft can provide comfortable and safe environment to let them to catch in order to let the next time space travelling passengers can feel satisfactory and enjoyable when they are catching the space tourism leisure's spacecraft to fly to anywhere in space.

In general, the expectation of factors space passengers include the following customer value elements, such as below:

- viewing space and the Earth.
- experiencing weightlessness and being able to float freely in zero gravity.
- experiencing pre-flight astronaut training and related sensations.
- communicating from space to significant others.
- being able to discuss the adventure in an informed way.
- having astronaut like documentation and memorabilia.

These objectives need to be combined with, sometimes conflicting constraints, such as guaranteed safe return, limited training time, reasonable comfort, and minimum medical restrictions. All these above issues which will be every space travelling passenger considerate matters before they choose the space tourism leisure company to catch its spacecraft to fly to space. So, all these factors will influence the next time space passenger number. Any space tourism leisure company can not neglect how to solve these all matters before they decide when their next time space tourism journey to be achieved.

Consequently, if the space craft tourism leisure company could revise what aspects of its last space tourism journey to find what are its wrong or weakness or unattractive challenges to cause any one space travelling passenger who feels unsatisfactory. Then, it can have more effort to concentrate on improving

its next space tourism journey to raise its space tourism service performance level , e.g. people, food, leisure etc. service aspects and its space tourism product quality level, e.g. proving comfortable spacecraft facilities to let space travelling passengers to catch in whole spacecraft tourism journey. Then, it will have more confidence to achieve the raising space travelling passenger number when any space tourism entetainment providers can apply (AI) technology to assist their space tourism mission development.

- What is the prediction space travelling passenger desire method ?

The prediction space travelling passenger individual desire method can be one survey investigation method. When every time spacecraft finishes space tourism journey mission, after all space tourism passengers catch the spacecraft to arrive earth from space. When they arrive earth space station destination, then the space tourism leisure company can arrange survey investigation staffs to enquire their feeling for this time space tourism journey immediately.

The survey content can include as below:

Do you feel satisfactory or unsatisfactory to which aspects of this time space tourism journey?

(1) On service aspect questions include as below:

(a) Do you feel space food taste is good?

(b) Do you enjoy this time space tourism journey arrangement?

(c) Do you feel satisfactory to space staff

service performance?
(d) If you have unsatisfactory feeling for any one of above questions, which aspect issue cause you feel unsatisfactory to explain to let us to know in order to us to revise our service performance.

(2) On product aspect questions include as below:
(a) Do you feel comfortable when you are catching our spacecraft in whole space tourism journey?
(b) If you feel comfortable , may you explain the reasons what aspects of our spacecraft has weakness to cause you feel uncomfortable?
(c) Do you feel safe when you are catching our spacecraft in whole space tourism journey?
(d) If you feel unsafe, may you explain the reasons what aspects of our spacecraft has weakness to cause you feel unsafe?

Finally, we thank your ideas to be given to let us know how to improve our every time future space tourism journey in order to find what challenge cause our service performance and product quality which can not satisfy your needs. So, we shall improve to avoid future challenges continue occur.
Our mission is achievement of 100% satisfactory level to our every space travelling passenger individual feeling. Also, we hope that you can choose our space tourism leisure service again, when you have another time space tourism leisure desire need. However, we shall revise to improve our service performance and product quality to be better, after collecting your ideas from this time survey investigation. I think you spend time to give your ideas from this survey investigation faithfully.
So, survey investigation method will be one important idea gathering tool to help any space tourism leisure company to revise the weaknesses to raise or improve future every time space tourism journey service performance and product quality to achieve raising competitive effort in this new space tourism leisure market.
Hence, survey investigation method will be the best idea gathering

method to predict how space travelling passenger emotion or desire need will change in order to achieve the objective of raising every time space tourism journey future space travelling passenger number more easily for every space tourism leisure company.

- The prediction of price factor influences space traveler number

The space tourism leisure organizations indicate the total cost of a trip into space is rapidly coming down from the initial price level of about US$600,000, it is obvious that the space travelling customer base is going to be rather small. Typical customers tend to belong to the top 1% income bracket. They also indicate that the price comes down , it is expected that new space travelling customer groups will enter the space tourism leisure market.

Typical new customers include people in other brackets with one-of-a kind incomes, such as inheritance or business sold. There are indications that those types of customers are becoming interested in spending on an once-in-a lifetime space experience. Therefore, the growth of the space tourism market is highly sensitive to customer satisfaction and how it is communicated through various media.

This will establish the status factors of space tourism and corresponding brand reputation service providers. They also suggest that any operator monitors space travelling customer satisfaction closely, as it will help developing increasingly accurate estimates of how the space tourism leisure market will develop.

Hence, it seems that every time space tourism journey price variable factor will influence the time space tourism of customer individual leisure desire and the space tourism passenger number. For example, the minimum price goal foe a variable space tourism business is currently estimate to be below US$3000-4000/kg for a round -trip depending on variable configuration and operation size. At this price, they estimate that somewhat over 1 % of the high income earners are potential customers.

However, for significant volume growth the longer term goal should be below US$2000/kg for a typical passenger, baggage and supplies. The lower price will probably open space tourism to a broader population, expanding the customer base and altering expectations. beyond this point space tourism will become into a travelling competitive leisure commodity, price competition will ensure and service providers need to rethink their space tourism marketing and branding and price strategies.

I shall also recommend how to attract the potential customers successfully. First, space operators need to pay special attention to the right level of customer services. Second, various preparatory customer operations cost, such as a travel to the launch site, space tourism destination accommodation, pre-flight training, medical check-ups and equipment my add up to between 10 to 15 % of the actual space travel cost. Thurs, solving the right balance between services offered and cost of client operation in order to earn the largest intangible benefits, such as loyalty, confidence, leisure enjoyment, comfortable space travelling journey as well as tangible benefits, such as profit, spacecraft manufacturing facilities, space stations, space hotels , space swimming pools, space gardens, space cinema etc. which are built to similar to earth building facilities to satisfy space travelers‘ needs.

- The prediction of price factor influences space traveler number

The space tourism leisure organizations indicate the total cost of a trip into space is rapidly coming down from the initial price level of about US$600,000, it is obvious that the space travelling customer base is going to be rather small. Typical customers tend to belong to the top 1% income bracket. They also indicate that the price comes down , it is expected that new space travelling customer groups will enter the space tourism leisure market.

Typical new customers include people in other brackets with one-of-a kind incomes, such as inheritance or business sold. There are indications that those types of customers are becoming interested in spending on an once-in-a lifetime space experience. Therefore, the growth of the space tourism market is highly sensitive to customer satisfaction and how it is communicated through various media.

This will establish the status factors of space tourism and corresponding brand reputation service providers. They also suggest that any operator monitors space travelling customer satisfaction closely, as it will help developing increasingly accurate estimates of how the space tourism leisure market will develop.

Hence, it seems that every time space tourism journey price variable factor will influence the time space tourism of customer individual leisure desire and the space tourism passenger number. For example, the minimum price goal foe a variable space tourism business is currently estimate to be below US$3000-4000/kg for a round -trip depending on variable configuration and operation size. At this price, they estimate that somewhat over 1 % of the high income earners are potential customers.

However, for significant volume growth the longer term goal should be below US$2000/kg for a typical passenger, baggage and supplies. The lower price will probably open space tourism to a broader population, expanding the customer base and altering expectations. beyond this point space tourism will become into a travelling competitive leisure commodity, price competition will ensure and service providers need to rethink their space tourism marketing and branding and price strategies.

I shall also recommend how to attract the potential customers successfully. First, space operators need to pay special attention to the right level of customer services. Second, various preparatory customer operations cost, such as a travel to the launch site, space tourism destination accommodation, pre-flight training, medical check-ups and equipment my add up to between 10 to 15 % of the actual space travel cost. Thurs, solving the right balance between services offered and cost of client operation in order to earn the largest intangible benefits, such as loyalty, confidence, leisure enjoyment, comfortable space travelling journey as well as tangible benefits, such as profit, spacecraft manufacturing facilities, space stations, space hotels , space swimming pools, space gardens, space cinema etc. which are built to similar to earth building facilities to satisfy space travelers' needs.

SIX

THE INFLUENTIAL FACTORS PERSUADE TRAVELERS CHOOSE SPACE TOURISM

Nowadays, our earth is no longer an adventurous enough place for some experienced tourists. Space tourism will be a new sector of adventure tourism, which is in the near future will be fast becoming a new tourism leisure opportunity for experiencing the unknown. Of one day, space tourism is able to reach the mass tourism phase, due to improved safety and decreased operation costs, a future space tourist will possibly only need minimal training to cope with the zero cost.

Space tourism is quite well established with visits to space attraction and launch sites, and it is a wealthy trips to the international space station for any space tourism travelers. However, if any space tourism leisure companies can attempt to find what the most influential factors are to persuade travelers feel attraction more than travelling in our earth.

It aims to let travelers to choose space travelling more than earth travelling when they feel travelling leisure need. I shall indicate what will be the most important influential factors to persuade travelers to choose space tourism more than earth tourism as below: Firstly, I shall argue that the majority of different new space tourism journey destinations will be needed to find to satisfy different aged space travelers and different income space tourism consumers' needs. For example, the rich people have effort to consume longer time and reach any space tourism destinations where are far away from our earth of their every space tourism journey.

Otherwise, the middle income people will choose shorter space tourism journey distance from our earth and short time space tourism journey. Also, younger space tourism clients can accept more longer journey time, exciting fast speed spacecraft flying journey. Otherwise, old space tourism clients can only accept comfortable and shorter time safe space journey. So, it seems that safety, comfortable feeling, shorter time space tourism journey won't be one important influential factor to excite any young people who choose to consume space tourism leisure. Otherwise, safety, comfortable feeling, shorter time space tourism journey will be one important influential factor to excite any old people who choose to consume space tourism leisure.

Secondly, the another most important influential factor to excite space travelers to choose space tourism , it concerns whether the space travelers will feel what tourists benefits can be earned from a substantial variety of destinations choice. In general, space tourism with those of aviation, space travelers will hope space tourism will be travelling distances by air in a very short time, safely and comfortably, to bring them to arrive any space planet destinations when spacecraft reaches any space stations to stay in any space destinations.

Hence, space destination factor will bring important influential choice to any space destination journeys. As a result of the space technological tourism boom, the number of potential different space destination, choice attractions have grown with far fewer places on earth to which human do have access yet. However, the ultimate different space destinations to which many of us dream is not on earth, but as least 100 km above us, anywhere in space any planets.

If the space tourism leisure company can provide different space tourism destination choices to young or old age both space traveler target consumer groups. They will feel a real holiday when they will be able to enjoy a great image of the earth from planets. It might mean that every space tourism journey can provide different space tourism destination to let space travelers have another new travelling destinations where are far from our earth anywhere.

Hence, the different space tourism destinations will give them an unforgettable adventure. Think of how it would be to be able to check in at a " billion strategy" luxury hotel in space one planet, it means that the space planet destination can provide one luxury hotel to let space travelers to live one night or more in the space planet destination, how it would be to schedule the space traveler' vacation at one of the space tourism leisure company luxury resorts on the Moon or Mars.

This images seem from science fiction movies, but one should not forget that 100 years ago, the Wright brothers, aviation pioneers inventors and builders of the air plane, would not have imagined how, every day it is possible that future spacecraft can fly to any planets to let human have chance to stay in the space hotel one night or more.

Consequently, space destination choice and space tourism journey service performance, aviation safety, ticket price and leisure satisfactory feeling which will be important influential factors to attract future space travelers to choose space tourism leisure to replace earth tourism leisure in future one day.

SEVEN

Raising Space Tourism Leisure Consumption Strategies

Although, space tourism industry is a real enjoyment and exciting travelling leisure to human. It is possible that human will choose to consume space tourism leisure to replace earth tourism leisure, if human felt that earth tourism leisure is not attractive to them to consume to go to anywhere to travel in their leisure time.

But, I believe that space tourism industry has still many factors to influence human to choose to consume space tourism leisure, even they will consider space tourism leisure consumption I is only one time space tourism in their life time. Hence, space tourism companies ought achieve this aim to persuade or attract everyone prefer to spend space tourism leisure at least one time in their life, then it can represent success. However, I think to achieve this aim, it has these challenges to influence their success, even they believe space tourism leisure business is one potential attractive travel entertainment business. These challenges include such as:

expensive space tourism ticket price issue, catching spacecraft safe issue, space traveler personal body health issue, age issue, family and friend relationship influence issue, working time and holiday time arrangement issue, the space trip arrangement issue, weather issue etc. different challenges, which will have possible to influence every space tourism planner either who decide change to cancel the time space tourism plan, or forgive to choose space tourism leisure in their life forever.

Hence, how to raise space tourism leisure consumption desire will be one considerable matter for any space tourism leisure businessmen. I shall indicate my personal three aspect of strategical opinions to let them to know how to raise every space tourism planner individual space tourism leisure consumption desire to avoid every time space tourism passenger number will have decrease failure chance as below:

● (1) Strategic opinion

On the first aspect of strategic opinion, I feel that the space education tutor can teach new space knowledge to let every space traveler to learn any new space and earth knowledge during he/she is catching on the spacecraft in personal contact learning experience environment which can raise space tourism consumption desire. The reason is because the space tourism leisure traveler can raise extra space and earth learning knowledge when they can catch the spacecraft to fly and contact the space environment to learn and feel what the differences are between space and earth by himself or herself. Hence, it is very attractive to the space traveler student target group and I believe that their parents will encourage their sons or daughters to participate the time of space trip and they are more preferable to help them to buy the time space trip ticket, due to their sons and daughters can learn any space knowledge when they are studying. Moreover, every space traveler will feel surprise to learn any new space and earth knowledge from the space tutor's teaching, due to he/she is unknown that this space travel trip includes learning space and earth knowledge.

I suggest that the space tourism leisure businessmen can give learning opportunity to every travel trip space travelers to feel that this space actual environment can bring what disadvantages or advantages to influence our earth when they are catching aircraft to fly to space to travel in every space trip. The space and earth learning knowledge can include these two aspects of space learning knowledge and experience below:

On the teaching of space environment learning knowledge hand, the topics can include as below:

Firstly the space learning topic can concern how space environment influences water and hydrated minerals change , they can learn what our drinking water function how is applied to space environment. For example, in the space environment, they can learn and attempt to feel that how water can be used in protecting astronauts against harmful radiation from the sun and cosmic rays by cloaking spacecraft with a thin layer of water in the actual space environment as well as the space travelers can also feel water is same as fuel when they are catching the spacecraft, they can feel the water is heavy to transport into space when they are catching the spacecraft to fly to space during their whole space tourism journey. Moreover, when their spacecraft reaches anyone of planets and it stays on the planet's space station, e.g. Moon space station. They can learn how to attempt to contact the hydrated minerals to learn and feel what they contained in some asteroids may be possible sources of water and fuel in the actual space environment. When they are walking in actual space environment, such as Moon planet, they can contact or touch this hydrated minerals to learn how water molecules can be extracted and separated chemically to produce hydrogen fuel knowledge in the actual space environment. This is one exciting space learning experience to the space travelling student passengers.

Secondly the space learning topic can concern how human fights space threats , even when their whole space leisure journey, the space science teacher can let the space trip student passengers to feel that they are learning new space knowledge between the space science teacher and whose space trip student passengers. Such as how to protect our earth knowledge: Teaching them to know when will be threats to our earth from space. The space science teacher can explain how this space threating environment influences our life safety and let them to feel that a mass extinction can be triggered if an asteroid 10 kilometers across hit the earth. Even being the apex species in the food chain did not space carnivorous dinosaurs from such disaster, who knows if this terrifying scene won't happen before our eyes? So, the space travelers can image and feel how the space threating environment can influence their life safety in the actual space environment as well as the space science teacher can let whose space travelers to feel and image the actual earth disaster will possible happen suddenly to let they feel afraid in the actual space environment. Also the space science teacher can teach how our earth can fright the space stones attack to let the space traveler to know, when an impactor targets an asteroid for a controlled well-times wallop. The collision will change the asteroid's momentum, deflecting it from its original orbital path which intersects with that of the earth. So, at the moment, the space travelers can image they are a larger spacecraft near an asteroid which can also change the path. Given enough time, the gravitational pull from the spacecraft will be able to steer the asteroid away from the earth. So, every space traveler will feel that they are catching the spacecraft in the safe space environment to avoid the Earth disaster from space sudden unpredictable attack.

It is more fun real space tourism knowledge learning feel to let every space traveler has chance to learn any new space science knowledge when he/she is catching the spacecraft to fly to space to travel. Hence, one successful space trip ought include trip and learning experience both contents in order to raise every the space tourism planner individual space trip consumption desire.

● (2) Strategic opinion

On the second aspect of strategic opinion, space tourism leisure companies need to let planning travelers feel that anyone of space tourism leisure is very different to general tourism leisure. In general, tourism leisure is visiting at least one night for leisure and holiday, business or other tourism purposes in Earth only. Otherwise, space tourism leisure is other kind of an unique trip leisure or entertainment method, e.g. the space traveler can catch the spacecraft to visit any planets to stay to live at the planet's space hotel at least one night, e.g. Future potential populated Moon or Mars space hotel space trip. Moreover, the space travel companies ought give chance to let them to feel what weightless feeling is in weightlessness environment when they are walking on Moon or other planets in possible. Even, they can attempt to build these entertainment facilities, instead of space hotels, such as space swimming pools, space gardens, space cinema etc. building facilities. It aims to let them to feel what the differences between Earth and space life when they are walking on the Moon, when they are swimming on the space pools, when they are living in space hotels, when they are watching movies in space cinemas, when they are seeing flowers and different species of planets and fruits. e.g. oranges, apples, bananas, and vegetable and potatoes and tomatoes in space gardens. It is very exciting and fun space trip life experience between one days to seven days. So, they believe that they must not feel these space life experience if they do not choose to participate this time space trip planning journey by the space trip company preparation.

Also, due to that the space tourism passengers need to the pre-flight checks and training before they ensure to qualify to permit to participate the space trip. So space travel companies need to concern how to take care their health check and training matter considerately. It aims to let every space traveler will feel a market segment with fitness and extreme experiences as well as he/she will become popular with a market segment passenger to the space tourism leisure company, although he/she must not guarantee to pass the space training and/or pre-flight health checks to permit to participate the space trip. However, he/she can believe that he/

she is one worth space travelling passenger to the space tourism leisure company, even this time pre-flight health check or/and the short time space trip training requirements are failure. However, the space tourism leisure company must need to let all pre-flight health check and space trip training passengers to feel that it is only one space tourism which can give them and let customers view the space travel is as the ultimate showcase for health, even though a majority of the population can pass the pre-flight medical and other tests in order to raise their confidence and safety to catch the spacecraft to fly to space to travel when they are confirmed to pass these tests to permit to catch the spacecraft later.

In general, the expectations of future space passengers include the following customer value elements, such as below:

- Viewing space and the Earth.
- Experiencing weightlessness and experiencing pre-flight astronaut training and related sensations.
- Communicating from space to significant others.
- Being able to discuss the adventure in an informed way.
- Having astronaut-like documentation and memorabilia.
- Enjoying one exciting and fun space trip.

However, instead of considering these objectives need to be combined with, sometimes conflicting , constraints such as guaranteed safe, return , limited training time, reasonable comfort, and minimum medical restrictions. So, space tourism companies need to reduce every space traveler individual worries before they decide to make the time of space tourism journey. Then, it can increase their confidence to raise their space tourism consumption desire more successfully.

Consequently, instead of these consideration, a space travel operator must pay attention to the total customer experience over the entire customer process, starting from how the service is presented, proposed and sold. The service package must include training, instructions, travel to the launch site and various post. Travel activities to generate maximum customer satisfaction and brand building opportunity.

● (3) Strategic opinion

On the final aspect of strategic opinion, I think any space tourism companies space tourism companies need to consider every time space tourism ticket price and space tourism trip issues. It is important factor to influence every space traveler individual consumption desire. Due to space trip ticket price must be more expensive to compare common Earth trip travelling ticket price, so this kind of tourism leisure market target customer will be the rich and high income customer group.

On the space trip ticket challenge issue, despite that fact the total cost of a trip into space is rapidly coming down from the initial price level of about US$60,000, it is obvious that the customer base is going to be rather small and the client target customer is only high income or rich consumer group. Typical customers tend to belong to the top of the top 1% income bracket. So, ensures that space traveler number must be less than common Earth traveler number.

Also, such as the space trip ticket price, it is expected that new middle rich level or middle high level income customer target group will enter the space trip leisure market, when every space trip ticket price falls down about 1% Typical new customers include people in other income brackets with one-of-a-kind incomes, such as inheritance or business sold space traveler target group. These people will be space travel new client group, when its every space trip ticket price can be reduced to close 1 to 2 % nearly. If any space tourism leisure companies expect to attract new rich and/or high income target customer group to choose any one kind of space trip journey planning to consume.

These are indications that these types of customers are becoming interested in spending on an once-in-a-lifetime space experience. Therefore, the growth of the space tourism market is highly sensitive to customer satisfaction and how it is communicated through the various media. This will establish the status –factor of space tourism, and corresponding brand reputation of service providers. The minimum price goal for a variable space tourism business is currently estimate to be below US$3-4000/kg for a round-trip depending on vehicle configuration. So, space travel leisure companies need to concern every round space trip cost, it can depend on the space vehicle number and weight issue to influence every space trip ticket price variable to achieve how much it can earn.

On space journey design factor aspect, it includes these different facilities aspects how to design, because future space travelling consumers will concern whether the space travel company can provide special entertainment to satisfy their needs. The facilities include as below:

How to design space hotels to let them to live in comfortable space environment and eat the best taste and fresh food quality when the cookers need to cook in the space hotel in the space environment? How to design space swimming pools to let them to swim in safe space environment? How to design space sport centers to let them to run more easily in one space sport warm and safe environment? How to design one space garden to let them to see different species of Earth flowers, or plants? How to design one space farming land to let them to see different species of Earth fruits, vegetables, tomatoes, potatoes etc. fresh foods growth in warm and safe space farming land environment? How to design one space cinema to let them to watch movies in one safe and warm space cinema environment? All these facilities will be any one of future space trip's' important and attractive space trip leisure facilities to influence every space traveler to choose to buy the space tourism leisure company's space trip leisure service.

Instead of these space building entertainment facilities, they also need to concern how the space vehicle entertainment tools are provided the entertainment service to satisfy their needs. When the space travelers can sit on the space vehicles to move on any planets' lands, such as Moon. A number of space vehicle options exist in the market, mainly differing based on the seat capacity as well as the in-flight experience level offered. The typical space vehicle solution is a small, relatively light weight spacecraft taking between 2 to

10 passengers. The number of passengers depends on the service level, amenities and extra offered. The trip typically lasts about 10 hours and of which about 4 hours are spent in space. The main attraction is the weightless time after in space. The main attraction is the weightless time after re-entry has started. It is a rather low-G technology and therefore the medical requirements for participants are nor very high.

Consequently, the space vehicles, space leisure building facilities, the space trip reasonable price ticket level, every safe space trip journey arrangement, clean and fresh and good taste space food arrangement, space traveler individual real learning experience etc. these factors will be the main influential factors to raise the space tourism leisure company's competitive effort and the space traveler consumer individual consumption desire to the space tourism leisure company in the future.

Printed by Libri Plureos GmbH in Hamburg,
Germany